The Fate Motif

poems

Douglas Nordfors

Plain View Press
http://plainviewpress.net

3800 N. Lamar, Suite 730-260
Austin, TX 78756

Copyright © 2013 Douglas Nordfors. All rights reserved under International and Pan-American Copyright Conventions. No part of this book may be reproduced or distributed in any form or by any means, or stored in a data base or retrieval system, without written permission from the author. All rights, including electronic, are reserved by the author and publisher.

ISBN: 978-1-935514-83-1
Library of Congress Control Number: 2013952028

Cover art: *The Bayeux Tapestry* by unknown weaver
Cover design by Pam Knight

Acknowledgments
The following poems have appeared, sometimes in a slightly different form, in the following journals:
"Timeless" in *The Amaranth Review*
"Sweetbitter" in *Birmingham Poetry Review*
"A Day" in *Cream City Review*
"Old Color Photograph" and "1964" in *Dandelion Farm Review*
"Before the Breakup" and "The Half-Moon In the Window"
    in *Epiphany—epiphmag.com*
"At The Public Library" in *The Evansville Review*
"Buster Keaton and The Handkerchief" and "Elegy For the Card Catalogue"
    in *The Hampden-Sydney Poetry Review*
"When I Grow Up" in *The Monarch Review*
"A True Story" in *Natural Bridge*
"Leonard Woolf, March 29, 1941" in *Poet Lore*
"Admission" in *Poetry Motel*
"Lullaby" in *Poetry Northwest*
"Prayer Vigil For Interstate 81" in *Rockhurst Review*
"The First Time" in *Slant*
"Youth" and "Three Questions" in *Stickman Review*
"Home" in *The Sycamore Review*

Contents

The First Time

Lullaby	7
Old Color Photograph	9
Timeless	10
Elegy for the Card Catalogue	11
The First Time	12
A True Story	15
The Way I Remember It	16
Youth	17
Cathedral of Saint John the Divine, New York City	20
When I Grow Up	22
Before the Breakup	23
Baby Animals	24
The Fate Motif	26
Prayer (1)	28
1964	29

Endless

Song (1)	33
The Great Lakes Medieval Faire	34
Endless	36
Keith Douglas 1920-1944	38
Buster Keaton and the Handkerchief	40
Fact	43
Leonard Woolf, March 29, 1941	44
Stephen Crane in the Bowery	46
Wallace Stevens in New York City	49
Harmony	53
Listening to Mozart's Requiem Late One Afternoon	55
A Question	57
An Image	59
The Nature of Statues	61

Renewal

Song (2)	65
Adagio	66
Home	67
At the Public Library	68
A Day	70
Core	71
Three Questions	72
Sweetbitter	73
Her Grief	74
My Heightened Self	76
Admission	78
The Half-Moon in the Window	79
Wolf Feeding on Carcass	80
Prayer Vigil for Interstate 81	82
My Muse	84
Prayer (2)	85
Renewal	87
Notes	89
About the Author	91

The First Time

Lullaby

You cover your head with the sheet
and make a sound like a monster. I'm your mother—
I realize your lashes protect your eyes.
Take the sheet away from your face now.
I will sit here, my waist touching your leg,
until you can't hear my whispering.
You will wake up with my hands
in yours, though I will be downstairs,
with the sun, making breakfast.
When you were very little you asked me why
the kitchen is the only room in our house
that has sunlight. I asked you why
you didn't ask the sun. I don't remember
how you answered. You probably laughed.
Laughter comes easily to you. You see, our life together
is a bedtime story. You climb the pine tree
out back and put your question to the sun.
It opens its small mouth. It has no teeth.
I could swear the moon has holes in it,
like Swiss cheese…you remember that story…
the little mouse wants to eat the moon.
I'm so ignorant. I mean, I know nothing.
Tell me what the sun said, tell me
as you close your eyes and the dark unfolds,
revealing the sleepless, the deprived…
forgive me, I'm using my own language,
believing you understand me. Don't worry,
I'm not lonely. You're so young I'm still
giving birth to you. The moonlight will flood your room
when I'm not looking. I'll just happen
to wake up before you, and your presence

will comfort me even before you run down the stairs
and come into the kitchen. Go to sleep now.
The four walls close and open like a hand.
The window is an hourglass. There are stories
that can't explain these things. I tell them to myself
every day. Go to sleep now.
No matter how hard I close my eyes
I can't sleep. Something separates us. That's our nature.
And you accept me, I'm sure of it.
Balancing on two legs, I enter your dreams
and all night you will not wake for fear of losing me.

Old Color Photograph

Within the open
air of a carousel a man
is holding his daughter up
on the horse with the blue
skin and yellow mane.
They're not moving yet,
it seems certain.

He's wearing jeans and a jeans
jacket, she a pink dress.
The look in her eyes says
she's frightened. He's smiling
for no clear reason,
like an infant.

The sawdust, blonde as
hair, is there
to break their fall.
Soon, she will abandon
her fear, triple his smile.
They're revolving, with the earth,
around the sun, and waiting

for the small revolutions
that make a difference.

Timeless

All afternoon he looks at pictures of war in an old magazine.
His new life begins at dusk.
The sun won't burn anymore.
He's happy, the dead insist on happiness.
He wonders how they survived even one gray day.
His eyes are no good.
He thinks crying is for grownups.
He thinks babies never go to war.
The cherry tree moves closer to the long window beside the door.
Fear has six fingers, swallowed lungs.
He's not afraid.
Begins at dusk because the sun is a prophet.
At last pain dies.
But happiness is crazy.
After the explosion, after the dog tags are shaken out of the trees
his cat drinks from the toilet; after he separates his body
from the human body he brushes his teeth
and goes to bed and closes his eyes and opens his eyes
and cries for his mother just to see her against the darkness.

Elegy for the Card Catalogue

I'm a boy again, searching for the aisle I need.
Walking down it is like walking between low, gentle buildings.
I go all the way or almost all the way to the end,
stand on my tiptoes or crouch to reach the drawer
I want and slide it out like a safe-deposit box
containing a sandwich bag of marbles, a small collection
of little plastic Indians and the promise of knowledge,
each card at my fingertip, some soft and faded, some fresh and vivid,
some as captivating as history, some as young as my mother,
some as young as me.

All the titles sound so alike I can't decide.
I hold between my thumb and forefinger the card
that feels right, memorize the call number, slide the drawer
in, find the book and take it to where my mother is.
She remarks on it as if it's a precious artifact
I've brought back from a long journey.
We sit side by side, reading. My book
has paintings of headdresses and painted ponies.
And plenty of words, the beauty of which I need and want
to glean or hunt for.

I put the book down and go look to see
where I can find another one—my mother says there's still time.
A different aisle, the same soft brown wood, the same
number of drawers, the same little handles like fishhooks
handed to me, like scissors, the right way.
Before I stand on my tiptoes or crouch or stand
just the way I am and slide out another
safe-deposit box, mine, too, I run my eyes
along the highest ones, out of reach
but not forever.

The First Time

Have you ever seen *The Sound of Music?*
I know a woman who's seen it—oh Lord—
zillions and zillions of times. You should
watch it with her sometime. You can't just

say her eyes light up. You have to say
her eyes could power a small town, or
her eyes are the candles the citizens of
a small town gratefully kiss before lighting

when there's a blackout. The first time
she saw it was the year it was released.
She was six. One minute Julie Andrews
was twirling and saying the hills are alive,

the next minute Julie Andrews was a nun,
her face like a painting whose mouth opens.
But if the beginning was like Sunday School
gone a little crazy but still Sunday School,

the middle was the immediate answer
to a girl's sudden prayers. There, in front of her,
practically inside of her, was the mansion
her parents should have gotten instead of

that tiny house in that mean neighborhood.
Better yet: many possible brothers and sisters
in sailor suits and pleated skirts. Better yet:
Julie Andrews winning them over with her…

she couldn't have expressed it…her almost
palpable charm, teaching them in one fun lesson
how to sing. Better yet: Christopher Plummer,
mean on the outside, nice on the inside,

so strong she could have lived on his back,
so tall she could have seen the mountains
wherever she was, wherever he was. Oh
she could have laid her very own cheek

on the back of his neck and closed her eyes.
When the end was near, she couldn't have known it.
All her possible brothers and sisters—or
were they, now, her brothers and sisters?—

were standing outside a gate, asking a nun
if Julie Andrews could come back. Julie Andrews
came back…Christopher Plummer was nice
on the outside…their mouths touched, they sang

the same song. When the end was very near,
she couldn't have known it. She couldn't tell,
exactly, what was making her so scared.
A searchlight missed Christopher Plummer's face,

Julie Andrews and what were now her children
all hiding behind his back. A strange older boy,
his gun taken out of his hand, kept shouting…
then it was daytime and the whole family

was climbing a green hill toward the mountains.
She didn't know that they had lost their home,
that they were escaping a war. She knew,
she just knew, they were going on a picnic.

In a daze she followed her mother and father
and two brothers outside. There, across the street,
still open, all lit up, was the K-Mart,
and maybe because she wished for the first time

that her life could be a dream, or maybe because
she felt for the first time that her life could come true,
or maybe because after having sat and watched so much for so long
she herself could act, she burst into tears.

A True Story

Two girls dressed in blue
jeans and blue overalls scream

at a wall of trees, calling it
Jessica, pleading with it

to stop playing and come out.
No answer. They sit down,

one behind the other, on
dry grass. One takes a brush

from her pocket and gives it
to the other's poor hair.

Jessica laughs, where laughter has no friends.

The Way I Remember It

My brother and I went into the mountains to get away from people.
As we passed a young couple as we crossed a stream,
we wanted to kneel in the stream and float away.
We wanted to slip under the soil and become a skunk cabbage and
      pine trees.
We arrived at the lake after dark.
In the morning, we sat on a stone, obsessed
with the smoke from a campfire across the water.
We fled, following no trail, calling to the wind
to lift us up, frightening a doe, got down on our hands
and knees and crawled along a slender ridge.
I slipped and almost fell hundreds of feet.
We froze.
He said he would have gone after me.
I said we would have lain on the ground like a feather.
He said there would be no reason for him to live.
I said, Why are we so scared to live?
He said, Because I almost lost you.
I said, No, why is everyone so scared to live?
He said, Because I almost lost you.

Youth

In their right mind no one
now (if it's still there)
or 22 years ago
would ride (have ridden)

the subway all the way
from 116th Street
to 225th Street
in Manhattan to look

in a pet shop window,
but 22 years ago,
when I was 20
and into the idea

that thinking about death
is a passage to thinking
about birth, I did.
The truth is, I rode all that way

to see a friend, and on the way
to her apartment stumbled
upon the shop. And yet
substituting the shop

for her apartment feels,
even outside my mind,
like the actual truth.
In a small container

lay a litter of kittens
reduced to one who
looked through its blindness
at another person who,

like me, had stopped to see it
nudge and maneuver
within a phantom mass
of bodies an unknown distance

from their mother's belly…
to clarify, it was me it
alone looked at. And also
it looked at everything

around and above me—
the elevated subway tracks,
the pill bottle stopped right
at the edge of the gutter,

the half-filled, see-through, cage-like
metal garbage can—as
they drifted through the glass
into the heaving body,

its mouth and bones sizing
up and doing the trick
of refusing (for now)
great gulps of air…this image

simply can't be clarified.
Standing there, I was
as close to the object
of pity and love as

the sensations of pity
and love can ever be.
Even worse
than sentimentality

is dispassion, and
if I could have stood
on middle ground, I would have.
Someone not exactly

me, given that I had
experienced it myself,
doubted such a thing as
a good home, while the whole me

had (has now) a vision
not of hope,
but of something larger
we may live inside.

Cathedral of Saint John the Divine, New York City

Walking past the front steps of
this unfinished Gothic
cathedral begun in
1892, I'm inclined toward

nostalgia, I'm on my way
to sit still on the stoop
of an inorganic
building where I lived for

a year as a young man
and wonder why rain will
fall diagonally like wind and
stain the windows of

the cave where I've always lived,
why the sun, dark
orange, untouched, will
sink straight down, why

the forecast always calls for
absence, why today's calls for
heavy winds and rain late
this afternoon, and also

I'm on my way to
work to recall intervals of
joy, one of the forms
it came in—a woman's hand

late one night on my bare chest,
the bedroom window open
just enough for
us to hear a baby

naturally crying
in the next building, the woman
in a whisper and for
no reason saying,

"It's a very small baby"—
and many more now
unformed intervals that
wouldn't feel the same if

they ever got under my skin
and transpired in me
again. And spent joy
doesn't actually graze

like grass the surface of
my ankles as I travel
the sidewalk to the seed of
1982, the cathedral,

now behind me, a replica of
raw history, gorgeous
all the same, the
scaffolding here and there

around the outside like flying
buttresses a breeze will
tear down without remorse
when the work is done.

When I Grow Up

I want to be an unpaid fireman, a pure
response to the negative,
and I want to stop fighting, lay my head
on the ashes.

When I grow up (I hear a man again
say somewhere, sometime
in the course of a downturned economy)
I want to be

the vein hitting the wall of my skin as someone
pulls me from the corner
and teaches me to dance like an amateur,
no money, no.

Haven't you
ever danced with yourself
at a small, useless party
celebrating no occasion?

I try every way
to remove my mask
save to reach all the way up through the poor muscles
in my human hand and remove it.

I, doused water,
will subside
like a dry wave one day, and no one
will be able

to look at me without feeling
the dead force with which
I wake in my arms
and go to work.

Before the Breakup

The second movement of Spring made us cry.
At intermission, in the filled concert hall
lobby, we stood alone. In so many words,
we said we could feel Vivaldi
walking up to us and breaking our skin
and never arriving. Four seasons, each
with three movements, were gone along with
the candles dripping with old tears we held up
to our eyes in the middle of Spring, the
period striving for grace, death, and life.

I forget what the orchestra played next.
Maybe before they played it, they formed a half-
circle, and bowed to us whom they had moved,
basking in the sound of four hands clapping.
Whatever happened, after the music began
a second time, we sat together, and
in listening lost ourselves: not even
childless minor composers, not even
by a few good strains
survived.

Baby Animals

to Beverly Goodrum

The way certain kinds—horses, giraffes, zebras,
elephants, you name it—emerge small and whole,
immediately ready, on unready legs,
to walk, should provide little or no
fuel for sentimentality.

There's already an immensity
to their lives that, it seems, they can't bear,
as if a cumbersome half-moon will soon
visit them in their much need for sleep
and slowly herd them away from a fortified
circle of peace. And the way certain kinds—

dogs, skunks, prairie dogs, foxes, you
know the names—exist prostrate in a mass
of brothers and sisters, humble barriers
of raw skin touching, for sentimentality
should also provide little or no fuel.
They're already prophetically dispersing,
hunting far and wide for original contact.

And yet in the deep dark of our comprehension
we savor them, cooing and aahing
over them in pictures or real
eye-pictures, unable to keep mute
about how cute they are, our hearts skipping
and sticking to a nursery rhyme beat, as if
we're infinitely infant adults
with four legs and four arms, both of us

like a twin separated at birth, our climate
crossed with rays of light like
the bars of a crib, no one in pity
over us, looking down.

The Fate Motif

How was the concert two tourists didn't attend
lived through, and lived through, before the final last
note struck? Just one of the greatest symphonies played
by an Oxford College orchestra who will soon fast
go to seed, out in the real world...

Instead, the two tourists just walked the old streets,
hearing scores of young voices keeping each other
afloat under the May sun—the partial world complete.
One tourist was a man, and the other was his mother.
After four efforts, Beethoven's Fifth

entered Beethoven's mind, emanating from a theme—
for its originality there were no words.
But much later, long before one mother dreamed
that birth could free her son,
someone coined a phrase: "The Fate Motif":

~~~

three short notes followed by a long one.
The man could hear it in the young voices in the May sun
the dusk held in its eyes in bursts, and then longer than possible.
The mother could hear it in the Evensong
attended neither by her son nor her, in the cathedral
near the meadow, and the river they never walked on or along—
how is the unreal world lived through,
before it's over? Into the cathedral the question withdrew
as they flowed toward the whole accessible meadow.
"Never" doesn't matter. Many people
have walked along the river, and many will—many mothers,
many sons, many students and priests
and doctors and teachers and lawyers and saints,
each one no less than the others
the last one, and the first.

Prayer (1)

Heaven was born without incident. And then
the idea of earth appeared
to a deity to be necessary.

It took several days to amend heaven.
And then there was light
everywhere, and nothing to contrast

light to, save moonlight. There was light everywhere.
And then over billions of years
a deity gradually

handed down to us a hollow,
and with our secular fire taking in lost
moonlight, causing ingenuity

and unnatural, natural
trouble, we will find our own method
of breaking down and reawakening dew, one day

we will prefer bringing cruelty to a close
over fearing for the newly born. Amen.

1964

The boy sits still as his mother brushes
his long brown hair, then takes the excess
in her hands, twists it into a bun, and

pins it. It doesn't matter to her if his eyes
are brown or dark green. She insists they're both.
Essentially, the morning sun flying

through the small window is the afternoon sun.
She says, "All right, we're done." Now the heads
of his school will accept him, a good boy

who's still himself. Notebook in hand,
he begins the walk. The end of the world
is around the corner, and he'll survive, just as

he could've survived the ice that was the age of the world
way before Columbus discovered America.
Will today be the day he'll learn about

the long black hair pierced with feathers?
Later, school over, the walk home over,
in the small room next to the kitchen, as

his mother takes out the pins, a waterfall—
it's no dream—in midair
begins.

Endless

Song (1)

after Boris Pasternak

When it was Desdemona's time to sing,
her finger began to ache, and the pain
spread like a fan through the four remaining,
while her other hand waited in the wings.

A fury in his words made true love false,
doused the spent match, seduced the peace moth,
annulled the flame, and blasted the willow,
willow, willow of bliss to final sleep.

When it was Ophelia's time to sing,
the way to Heaven became steep and thorny,
and the way to Earth, already traversed,
terribly easy, withered inside her.

A madness in his words sucked the honey
from her mind, turned kindness unkind,
and song hollow, with rosemary for remembrance,
pansies for thoughts, and violets for death.

Flying and flying out of all that grief,
they entered the universe and saw that it was
heartless, unwieldy, incredible, and because
it spoke their names, pitiable, light, believable.

The Great Lakes Medieval Faire

Two mounted, armored
knights in a clearing removed
from the maidens and jesters
and booths and goods go backward—
not in time—as they plunge
toward each other and
cross swords.

Counterfeit violence
recedes like the gathering
clouds.

Light
from the eclipsed
sun that was created
ex nihilo and is to there
returning via a
densely vegetated
artery through a wall
of contiguous trees
strikes two costumed horses
on every muscle
on their bare necks.

Such is
hope for the future: going through
the motions of
stagnation and therefore
not constrained by probability.

Whether to hope
does any good is
a moot question—
its value is a
smooth blade that even
in the throes of extreme
simulation won't rain
into flesh.

The clash resounds
as the logic branches
twice into the same bounded bloodstream.

Endless

for Keith Jarrett

Entrance

The daughter of a man named John Graves
put down on paper all the details
of his several visits many years earlier
to his Amherst relatives, the Dickinsons.

All the details, like the whole of life,
bear fleshing out, one in particular.

First Phase

In the guest room,
Graves, sleeping, before time
summoned the sun, heard sounds
withdrawing into his released eyes—rising
from the piano downstairs.

And was awakened
by nothing he knew—
by a method succeeding
in not shrouding the notes—not
a method at all.

Second Phase

"I can improvise better at night,"
Emily explained in the morning.

Endless

Fleshed out, to improvise means to remain
in the continuum while conceiving
seasoned leaves and realized, flowerless
roots and a circle and its perfect center
through which circumference unencumbered flows—

unspeakable only if the name itself,
"Emily," bore eyes and a mouth, only if
"nature" begets outside consciousness
while giving its own to birth and beyond.

In the flesh, he, John, listens always
to her explanation always leading back
to her impulse—the night with no motive,
the original night, the middle name

with a crevice in its fissure
through which the imaginary, unsung
ego sinks.

Third Phase

The morning
went on, outgrowing itself—replenished within
its metaphorical progression of keys
at the touch of thoughts quicker than blood's reach
to the brain.

Keith Douglas 1920-1944

"Remember me when I am dead
and simplify me when I'm dead."

Imagine experiencing two years
of intermittent combat in North Africa,
and then joining the D-Day force, and being killed
three days into the Normandy invasion.

What war did to him is difficult
to say. His war poems are not quite sorrowful,
not quite graceful, reject easy
mourning, but not murky, intricate

pity—for whom or what? For the horrors
human beings are so capable of, which
skillful language somehow echoes,
or so I believe he believed.

In a poem he never finished, he tries
to explain that what allows his brain
to explore "constellations of feeling"
is "a beast on my back." "Words are

my instruments but not my servants,"
begins a poem he wrote in Egypt
while recovering from wounds to his right foot,
right calf, left arm and left shoulder. In France,

a shell exploded in a tree above him.
The tiniest of fragments must have killed him.
There was not a single mark on his body,
but I can't simplify you, I'm sorry.

It's necessary to treat war with language
as forged, as wrought, as his. How unsettling
to find in his poems brutality brilliantly
described rather than merely argued against,

but to read his poems is to get at all of war,
from its one remaining bone to its excess flesh to its whole soul
subject to substance. We can only know
what we truly understand, they seem to say,

we can only put an end to what we truly know.

Buster Keaton and the Handkerchief

In *Sherlock Jr.*, the great comedian
swipes a handkerchief from a crying woman
and dabs his eyes. I won't try to explain
why taking something from someone without
asking seems at that fluid moment in the
then new miracle of motion pictures like
the perfect thing to do. And I won't say
why tears abound. You've probably seen the film
or will some day. I won't give it away.
In the spirit of the silent era,
I don't want my words to be heard, but
displayed: little torn white flags against
a black background. If Keaton were alive,
and he is, in a way, he would see
right through my lies. His images are
essentially childlike, wildly mortal,

sacred. Who finally gets the handkerchief?
They're crying because money is scarce—
that's all I'll say. Children take without asking,
but would they watch this scene and laugh as if
at themselves? The whole film is slightly unnerving.
When Keaton, who plays a projectionist,
falls asleep, then walks out of his body
and into the screen, it's impossible
to say where we are, though we're glad we're there.
In the film within the film, he's a detective
who can solve anything. He wakes from the dream,
but moments later a love scene he can't
walk into teaches him how to kiss
the girl who's climbed to the projection room
to tell him she's discovered he's innocent.
(I've given it away.) Innocent of what?

Stealing her father's watch. But to me
innocent of self-doubt, inner despair,
outward silence. (I want to be heard.)
Perhaps those who've seen the film interpret it
exactly the way I do. Perhaps my
deepest feelings are borrowed. I read once
that Keaton, during the filming of *Sherlock Jr.*,
broke his neck performing a stunt and lived
with it for ten years until a doctor,
during a routine physical, discovered
what had happened. I say Keaton's films
illuminate the human mind, which is
the star I wish upon, and try not to kill
the human body, which is the star I wish for…
may blood never stop exiting the heart
and coloring in the veins. It's hard

to forget that stunt: water from a huge pipe
comes down on his head, dousing him. The water
shuts off. He reappears. It's supposed to be
funny. It's not. It's stunningly beautiful.
I think all my gut reactions to art
are dead wrong. But Keaton always claimed
his talent was completely instinctive.
From the time he could crawl, one feature
of his parents' vaudeville act was his father
lifting him up in the air and throwing him
against a wall. The audience refused
to see it as real, broke into laughter
because Buster's face showed no pain, nothing.
His father told him not to, so she didn't.
In the films he made, he went on wearing
that blank expression (except in one scene),

hoping for laughs. "I couldn't even whimper,"
he once said about those vaudeville years.
Actually, he took an imaginary
handkerchief from his father without
asking, erased his grief and, years later,
filmed something like it so that something like
reality would stand before our eyes.
He cast his father in *Sherlock Jr.*
He plays the father whose watch is stolen,
who perceives guilt where innocence abounds.
But the ending is happy. And the film
is immortal. At any given moment,
Buster Keaton, The Great Stone Face,
in need of a handkerchief, swipes one
from a crying woman. Then she swipes it back.
Then he swipes it back. Then she swipes it back.

This will go on for as long as there are tears.

Fact

I love it that Queen Elizabeth I wasn't
a morning person,
every day rose long after her countless servants,

the ones she trusted standing patiently by her
bed, or just outside
the room, waiting for the life beyond the royal life

of sleep, wishing, perhaps, to go back to bed
themselves, with no one
around them, trusting just themselves. Oh how some facts

inspire endless speculation. Did the extra sleep
give Elizabeth
the edge she needed to keep her nation standing,

or did her life's work quite simply wipe her out?
I see her with closed,
strife-torn, language-enriched, blood-tinged, Shakespearean

eyes through the dreamless, less than peaceful future
with its morning sun
that will one day let me close my closed eyes. Endless.

Did she wake each day content that she had stretched the peace
beyond the worlds
of politics and fate as long as she could stretch it, or was

every waking minute peace made flesh, earned between
a servant's dawn
and a Queen's? Oh how some facts are so good

as to not deliver us from mystery.

Leonard Woolf, March 29, 1941

> *"The house has lost its shelter."*
> Virginia Woolf, *Between The Acts*

He stands on the lawn, looking out over the valley.
I believe he believes
he's clutching the note she left, though it's inside
the house. "Everything has gone from me
but the certainty of your goodness."
One day has passed since she drowned herself. Her mind
will go no more from pure
sanity to out of nowhere
illness and back again.
She had sensed a wholly devastating surprise
coming and refused to let it show its latent face.
He stands still, surpassing perfect misery.
"I begin to hear voices
and I can't concentrate. Everything has gone from me…"

Would you believe he thinks of the trouble she had
finishing her novels? The trouble any novelist
might have who cares more for detail (how
one wing of a butterfly pausing over
a rosebush would appear to a person
plagued with loneliness more spectacular
than the other), than for narrative (where
the butterfly flies off to). "I can't read.
What I want to say is I owe all my happiness to you."

When the war began, a Nazi victory
seemed possible, even likely, and they supplied themselves
with poison, stood on the lawn one day
and watched bombs intended for the cement works
hit the river bank. A few days later
there was an abnormally high tide and a strong wind…
the bank gave way and flooded the valley.
She lived to see it dry again. Then used the river.
I believe he feels if he opened his mouth
and turned his tongue from stone into flesh, his lips
would taste like the war still going on, falling on his head—
would it feel like anything at all? In time—
let's believe—he'll stop believing
she owes all her happiness to oblivion.

Stephen Crane in the Bowery

To be poor among the poor or to be
rich as a red sunset, he arrived
in New York City in the late fall
of 1892, his Civil War novel yet to be,

his inner war allayed, mitigated
by how the singular way he took stock
of the empirical cut through the assault—
at any rate, going nowhere—on his senses:

clangor of bells on red
and brass cable cars; roar
of elevated trains; horses;
drivers with whips; pavement

and hooves meeting face
to face; conviction (absorbed
completely by he who built more
than hearing into all there was

to hear) in the sound of eye-
despair surrounding
players of hand-organs;
tailors, peddlers, dressmakers

and menders of opera-
glasses (the nearer he grew
to unconditional reality,
the more he saw what it is

an artist is—the factual
and the fictional being
stranger than ground
constructed from the ground up);

the unveiled, if mute (no
visible sentiment
in his way with words,
and a sorrow so deep

it undermined the ravages
of hope) physiognomy
of the little chapel between
two apartment buildings;

odor of beer in the auras
surrounding beer salons; vacant
lots dotted with small
hoodlums (the opposite

of the employed, who had
not the courage to stand still);
rooms for 10 cents; rooms
for a charitable 5 cents and

coffee and bread in the morning;
rooms like dens; people like wolves
directing their undirected
misery onto the pack (theology

said wealth doesn't translate
into happiness); white-as-sleet
light from the streetlights, and in time
the summer sun like the nation

with its head in the clouds
looking down on giant life
problems (impressionism
was where his imagination started up,

and not ended up). He held the fabric
between the Bowery and its curiosity—
lacking compassion and with it a sense
of unfairness—about itself (its correct

proportion he was).

Wallace Stevens in New York City

Before

soft Connecticut. Before he was
insured in life and work,
his real work perhaps taking place,
in effect, in a past life.
Arguably genesis
of the intelligence almost
covering the flesh of his poems with crystal bones.

City of men
and women. City of a young man
whose solitary as well as
individual perception arrived
there five months into
the 20th century.

Fragments. Flashes.
Not exactly where and in what
small room
he lived, or whether
he looked for work,
but from what vantage point
he saw his surroundings.

Vulgar city, electronically
charged by necessity. Still,
a stranger, a man, sitting
with a cat on his lap
in a chair outside of a saloon
on 6th Avenue and 11th Street.

The real man. And the felt man.
Church bells and voices of children
as if not, in fact, infused
with the lifeless faces
of buildings, and the man
near the Washington Square Arch
in rags on grass, sleeping.

And he himself
walking. Walking until he reached
a spot where he could see,
in the narrow
space between
two buildings, the sun setting.

People on street corners shooting craps. The stars
in his eyes going home
(a boarding house run by two
unmarried French women) to read
poetry, his eyes falling inward,
his mouth silently telling
the rest of his body to go to hell.

And where was that?
Walking, always. To Madison Square
and the statue of Diana, her eyes
hunting over everyone's heads,
on the top of the tower
of the building called "Garden."

Up 5th Avenue. Past the 5th Avenue
Hotel and the Dewey Arch,
all the way to the cold
and beautiful St. Patrick's Cathedral.
Bicycles and street-organs.
Art galleries and exhibitions.
Impersonality all around him.

And his emotion and intellect
like two arms embracing. Walking
to the small funeral
of Stephen Crane, exactly
at the Central Metropolitan Temple
on 7th Avenue near 14th Street.

Back outside afterward. The shaky
hearse rattling off into the distance
as if shaking the cobbles of the street.
Few passers-by noticing.
Walking to Trinity Church
and Astor Library, and Low Library
at Columbia University.

Roses and evergreens around the third
he saw. And song-sparrows heard.
From all this, inimitable, preceding
him, he descended or rose
because what it brought to him
he brought to it.

Excursions. Always
excursions back and forth.
Stability in the home nowhere
in the middle of the axis
of the axiom that the eye
is destroyed by brutality
and beauty.

Unless the eye finds the locus
of each. Turns its back on two buildings
and the imaginary sun
to see the actual horizon
where
Diana dies

and lives.

Harmony

In November 1916, Marcel Proust,
to prove that an idea worth living
was feasible, hired a string quartet
to play at his apartment.

Inside his walls lined with cork (to shelter
his ill-health and brittle peace from world-sounds,
and not to build a universe of unsurpassed acoustics)
he lay on his bed above

portions of his manuscript in wild
disarray among neat stacks on the floor.
Like invisible, unimaginable,
unstruck nerves, the four appeared,

only the cello a vast body and neck,
even that manageable, and charmed the emptiness
into D Major, César Franck a deity
composed of a man composed

of sheer sensuous sound who doubtless
disbelieved in organic form come to an end.
Proust's words: "Would you do me the immense kindness
of playing the whole work again?"

Again D Major, like a new course of treatment,
again as the work progressed D Major charmed
into other keys, unlike before continuing to be
the source, the seed-bearing

idea painted on all walls outside
his own, the allegory beyond the cave.
An hour after midnight at the absolute beginning.
And now he is nowhere,

in the present tense, in the inception of time
time itself conceals, lying on his bed,
his eyes on the ceiling, on the colorless
flower that will be there,

though there
won't be an echo of the reprise.

Listening to Mozart's Requiem Late One Afternoon

My ears do all the work.
I can't see weeping.

My elbows touch my desk.
The tips of my fingers

touch my forehead.
The edges of my hands

don't quite meet.
I see a slice of light.

The tips of my fingers can't
hurt anything in this room,

the CD player, the CD,
the books, the windows.

I can't sink through the floor
passing for the ground

or rise through the ceiling
passing for the sky.

I can't see weeping.
The music says all

things beautiful create
for themselves a hell

through which to progress
note by bone, muscle

by texture, sinew
by sinew, says

long after who I was died
I became who I wanted to be.

A Question

April, 1941. Hampstead, London.
A place in the world in the at times
unforgivable past. Stephen Spender—he lived past
all the Nazi air raids until his death
in July, 1995—wrote after the war
of how one night a bomb fell
on the house across the street from the house
where he and his wife, Natasha, pregnant, lived.

What did he do?

Natasha, perhaps because of the core,
the pre-hush inside her, showed no fear.
She couldn't be saved any further.
He ran down the stairs—they lived
at the top of the house, in a garret,
one room of which from the widening,
weakening impact of the removed event
merely lost its ceiling, mere rubble, as opposed
to cold, cold rain, raining down—
and found the house across the street
gone completely.

What did he do?

There was no one to save, despite the clanging bells
of the fire engines in the encroaching distance.
He began walking, and walked for miles
through the empty streets as if running
opposable thumb bones down the spine
of the standing structures on either side of him.
Walking was doing, but was he really doing
anything? He recalled the sound, before the bells—
the comparatively soft clanging—of the impact,
like a train emerging screaming from a tunnel.

What had he thought?

That the end of the world that he had
anticipated since birth had arrived—
the wrong thing to think, he knew, but thinking itself
wasn't wrong. What did he do? For already
measured miles he walked, thinking and feeling
alive, thinking of the dead faces
over the masks of political systems
that need not commit terrible acts,
but do, and of the dead tears falling from faces,
their shining mouths inside the core, the after-hush
of the end, to him alone saying, "Be spared, do
or be good, and rejoice in thy neighbors' love."

An Image

War abhors individuality.

To support such a statement all I need
is an image on the Bayeux Tapestry:

two of William The Conqueror's soldiers
setting fire to a house as a young woman
and her young son appear to pause, on
their way out, on the threshold, the two

soldiers depicted as giants in comparison
to the victims, though all four were victims,

it could be said, of the immense machinery of war.
I want to forget the giants in the eyes of the artist.
They're the ones getting payment and glory,
employing fire as a weapon, shadowing

each other in age and strength, neither one
more ruthless than the other, canceling

each other out. In my eyes they disappear,
and I can see the terror in the uncaptured
pores on the skin on the face of a single
individual who's given birth to another.

The ground under her feet is a dark
wavy line, like a child's drawing

of the top edge of a cloud smashed into
the ground. Her body, save her face and hands,
is covered with a dark frock, one of her hands
alive and empty, her other hand grasping

a small hand alive with flesh and blood.
Her expression? Human bewilderment

reduced to one human, and expanded,
according to pity and irony, to one human,
until hope is the lonely and gritty word
it was when first uttered. Pausing on

the threshold, she is not yet homeless, in
her mind, it could be said, the bitter world

has not yet refused to take shelter inside
the love inside her body. War abhors
safety, elemental or created, real
or imagined, as wood worships fire and

ashes ashes.

The Nature of Statues

A crowd flows over Westminster Bridge,
in the lifelike light of May, under
the actual sky, past the unmoving,
clearly unmoving, statue of Boudica,

Celtic woman warrior, and her two daughters,
in a chariot drawn, not at the moment,
by two rearing horses, at the moment
no one holding the reins, Boudica, Queen

of the Iceni, who gathered tribes together
against the Romans, her daughters cowering
behind her, one of her hands gripping a spear,
her other hand raised to the sky, her looming,

bloodless presence casting doubt on the ever-
living crowd, and perhaps on the lonely fact
that the revolt was brilliantly successful,
and then was brutally crushed, Boudica

inspiring awe in her followers, and then
sacrifice, and then taking her own life.

A crowd flows over Westminster Bridge, so many,
who would have thought death would spare so many?
The far distant past can't come close
to inspiring such a question, and so the far

distant past is its own country, and so
sacrifices itself for itself, all the time
waiting, perhaps not in vain, for its own sun
to rise, while blood rushes from an uncarved heart,

sending a message to dry eyes, and two daughters
are perhaps not cowering so much as
learning from the strength they don't yet possess
to not kneel, to not lie down, while one

lifeless hand raised to the sky, and countless muscles
inside the necks of two horses embrace May,
embrace snow falling down over Westminster Bridge
in real February, embrace June, March, November,

whenever 80,000 Britons were slaughtered
by Romans and pro-Roman Britons at the unknown
site of the decisive battle, after which
Boudica, still alive, felt wrong, and committed

that act one crowd after another flowing
past her doesn't remember her by, doesn't
need her to commit, and so, despite
that tremendous grief inside her, outside

the multitude, which can't be captured,
she doesn't go through with it. She lives.

Renewal

Song (2)

after Iris DeMent

When my morning comes around,
the moral of my story
will be placed at the beginning,
and I will go on reading
into my actions and my thoughts

anyway, looking to belittle
the conclusion I've come to
about myself and clothe myself
in a light that represents light
when my morning comes around.

When my morning comes around,
for a glaringly unknown
reason I will close
my eyes with my fingers
like a too late doctor,

and I will go on reading
my middle, my end, my mind
seizing itself as the moment
goes from loom to loom, and a bolt
of cloth becomes a spool of thread

when my morning comes around.
When the knot in my throat keeps rising.
When who I am springs from my lips, and I take it back,
and the knot is placed in my gut
when my morning comes around.

Adagio

Toward the end of the second movement of Gerald Finzi's *Clarinet
    Concerto,*
the clarinet starts to weep.

I hear it wrong
but something in me tells me I'm right,

and so perhaps Finzi desired the weeping
without wanting it.

I am human, and yet I don't
understand emotion.

I don't want sadness.
I want to walk to the kitchen

and wash my hands
without holding them under the faucet.

It seems as a human I have the power
to put eyes on anything,

and I can't understand it.
How do I become so sad I convince myself

I shouldn't breathe?
I wipe my breath away.

Meanwhile, the weeping goes on.

Home

Begin at the center, where you are not wanted.
Leave your house, start walking downtown, wait for the light
to find you, cross the street, let clouds form, rain fall—
everything is as it was before fear of sadness became sadness—
look down at your feet, up at the sky, wait for the light,
cross the street, lift your hand to your cheek, heal
the scratch, encourage the skin though it may die,
look in the windows at the toy soldiers, the fabric,
the unpainted mask, walk through the gas station,
the sign saying closed on both sides, remember
that if you move like a lung, expanding, contracting
you will continue to live, wait for the light, wait
for the light, cross the street as you might cross
a shallow river, feel like you have fallen through the crack
and are walking around underneath, stomp your foot
to test the ground, look up at the sky as if at the earth,
carry the darkness on your shoulders, wait like a ship in a bottle
for the wind to take it all. No wind. Begin again.
Open your door. Windows. Rip the curtains off your body.

At the Public Library

I stole a few glances at them.
I listened to them so
intently I lost interest
in the novel I was reading.
"Them" was a man
with a tweed jacket
teaching another man
with a light blue shirt
with his name stitched
in elegant cursive over the left breast how to read.

Elbows on the table, fingers
in his hair, the student
labored through an article
in The New York Times.
After several failed
attempts to pronounce
the word "deficit,"
he sighed, put down his hands
and started in on how
brilliant his wife is,
how she—I can't recall
his precise words—
developed an intolerance for his insistence on using her eyes.

The teacher, slow
to respond, at last said,
"My wife's begun to plead
with me to open myself
up and let some light in,"
or something to that effect.
I could have sworn
the novel I was reading

had become a novel about
a student who's never
felt he could walk
in the sun with his wife
holding brilliant hands,
and about a teacher
who's begun to believe
he can walk again
with his wife in the sun
holding brilliant hands,
begun to see he sees
words as flesh, complete
sentences as flesh
and blood, love as open to revision, perfect love as…

When I closed the novel and left,
they were still working.
Walking home, I read
the flawless sidewalk
as if to avoid the cracks,
read so deeply
into the moon it came closer
and closer to shedding
the two craters below the smooth forehead and developing true eyes.

A Day

It's a gray day. As I walk through the park,
I focus on a child who won't listen

to her father. In a bed of flowers she sits
Indian-style, touches the soil with her fingers

and paints a flat smile on her forehead.
Her father moans, lies back on the grass

and lays one arm over his eyes. He possesses
no anger. He can't move. He doesn't know

what to do. It's as if he gave the sun away
and kept his own flesh and blood.

I believe I know him. I believe we dress
in the same cold skin, a lifeline

slashed across each palm.
And we are only as beautiful as his daughter.

Her fingers must be the gorgeous color of soil.
Her forehead must not be blank. It's a day

without sunlight. It's a day
of hardship and imagination.

Core

Again, I look inside
myself, at the core
I lean on, and can't prove.

It's like leaning on
the earth on my shoulders,
like breathing with one

of the earth's roses
caught in and fitted to
my throat, a fragrance only

the only heart
shaped like mine senses. No,
it's like leaning on a

windmill on a weatherless
night, with my own
star riding above me, sinking

into my shoulders and my gut,
a promise kept and so
able to give of itself

again and again.

Three Questions

When I find all the reasons
the world is splendid, I set out
to find them again, and get lost
in spent effort, like an explorer
trudging in a small circle around
the north pole, looking up
into the echo of a fruitless plea.

Imperfect simile? I can't tell.
There's no secret of life,
except when what happens after
the secret of life is nullified
is examined. Suddenly,
territory is unknown,
bearings have no bearing.

I follow my small circle
of footprints, and discover hunger
is numb, a root stitched into
what was once upon a time
an orchard floor, into pale
earth strewn with apples with
no skin or meat or core.

Imperfect metaphor? Yes.
Emptiness is active, freezing
wind through the north star no one
who's broken their small circle
and set out for the starless
horizon can follow. Emptiness?
No proof of it will I ever find.

Sweetbitter

The instant I learn
a word I've used time
and again one way
was originally
used by Sappho the
other way around

a valve heart
opens in the air
around my body
within kissing
distance of an
ancient country

where lapse time
photography captures
a woman on a journey
from birth to death
putting one foot
behind the other.

Her Grief

Wishing to express her love
for swimming, I think: She walks
into the lake, head tilted
back, mouth open, the way one
walks into a cathedral.

She's up to her thighs in God
now, or at least that's what
the man lying on the sand
close to where I'm standing,
a Bible open on his chest,

would think. Last Sunday,
her grandmother—everyone
always said they were exactly
alike—died. The funeral
was yesterday. Last night,

she sped all the way back home,
no cops in sight, in tears.
Her friend, I've tried
and failed so many times
today to cheer her up.

A storm is threatening
to pass right over this lake
near her house, this lake complete
with a small beach that's about
to close. No more present tense—

this all happened years ago
when we who are still alive
were younger. There was no man
with a Bible open on his chest,
no chest to shelter from rain,

no lightning just yet, just a lifeguard
running right past me and right up
to the edge of the water to demand
she come in. She was up to her breasts
now, and now she was doing the crawl.

There was nothing anyone
could have said that could have
kept her from whirling, calm
as an underground fish, into the eye
of the lake. I prayed for her, I believe,

only after she started back.

My Heightened Self

My self barely
remembers that time
I lived a floor below
a blind woman, her seeing-eye
dog's tail sometimes wagging
against one of her apartment
walls like a foot stomping
to rouse my attention, no, her
attention, no, the attention
of my heightened self to whom my ceiling
was the blind woman's floor.

My heightened self, as abstract as
a man's heart comprising
a dog's soul, goes on emerging
like a womb out of that time, never
looking straight or sideways
at the blind woman's face, not knowing
exactly how her hair
and forehead (that my self
would see in the elevator)
survives like an eyelash
shyly looking down at a hand
tied to a sturdy leash,
not knowing how she walks through walls,
wherever she lives now,
from one end of her floor to the other
like an unsinking sun,
knowing she needs pity as much
as a dog needs to know
what the concept of kindness is
in order to be kind,

wishing to know what physically
limited human sadness
believes, and what in God's name that means,
and lastly, hoping
the woman who happens to be,
with the blonde flowers in her hair
the one color of spring,
with the winter coat (bright, bright gray
in my self's memory,
suspect, its eyes refreshed),
will never, ever, even if
with sentiment, and not
with sentimentality, wonder
how anyone can walk
from one end of their life to the other
with no one to guide them.

Admission

Why I love my life is always
on the tip of my tongue, my mind
in a fever to fashion
the exact explanation
out of the raw material

of language. And when I feel lucky,
why I love my life is always
a given, "my life" and "love" like
two pieces of semi-liquid
metal joined together before
I was born. And when I feel lucky,

I admit, I eagerly anticipate
the split, longing to feel once again
the tip of my tongue, the
delectable void I can never work hard enough to fill.

The Half-Moon in the Window

Looking out at my life so far, I wish
my human heart and every mistake
I've put into it won't fall away

and rise again clean and clear
and relatively shapeless:
the window in the half-moon.

Wolf Feeding on Carcass

This tug of war with this flesh, this
blood on this muzzle both
creates and
assuages

fear of living. Fear of death is dead,
as if it licked the eyes
of a lost
child, two

times licked the eyes before the child's
multiple paws became slices
of air, and
fingers. This

is Yellowstone National Park
after wolves were reintroduced
there,
to suffer

their hunger again, the answer right
there in a herd of elk, as if
tall tales time
and again

are zeroed to one that must be dragged down
and killed before it starves, while
child upon
child wanders

the towns and cities and backwaters
of this mandated country,
looking for
evidence

that dominion over each other
and peace through
mutual understanding are what people are
craving and hunting for.

Prayer Vigil for Interstate 81

I didn't attend, though I spend
six hours a week sandwiched between
tractor-trailers or shaken by the
breathless speed of passing cars. Help

always feels remote on this stretch
of America continually
vanishing into the distance,
today a light blue prison bus

parked along the side and an un-
even line of inmates stabbing
litter and lifting it into sacks
weighing down one shoulder. Help

also always feels close, a prayer
banished from the sky and zeroing
in on me who doesn't even
speak the prayer's language—sleek as the

voice on the radio between
compositions, between my terror
and my serenity, saying
the creator of that is Aaron Copland,

the creator of this is William Walton,
not telling the listener
how the music continually breaks out of
established patterns, suggesting

that when one emotion is born
it's because another emotion
is let go. At which point I'm
shaken by the breathless speed

of a passing tractor-trailer taking
live chickens to meet their destroyer,
little white feathers drifting
before my eyes, little dim signs,

too physical to be believed.

My Muse

There's a room inside a hospital
where I like to be born.

I put the same nurse there,
the one who my mother told me gazed
out the window and said,

"It's a good day to have a baby."
"Rain has a nurse's touch,"
is what the nurse's muse,
already alive in the next

day forward, and the next,
meant her to say. The doctor?
"Close your eyes, this won't hurt,"
he could have said, referring
to the rest of my life, meaning:

Due to noncircular
logic, unlike the sun,
that first breath keeps shining
through the window
shut for good and into my lungs,
sensing (no, imagining,

the cord being cut)
good tidings always.
And every time
those subsequent breaths
falter, my nurse
gathers the blood on my body
and puts it inside.

Prayer (2)

I'm downcast,
not knowing if
my eyes are glazed
with dew this late
in my life. The

dust I will be
means less to me
than the dust I,
not knowing, am.
Morning in my

wrist breaks in two,
doubles the one
footprint earth asks
me to leave. Are
ideas true?

I, not knowing,
must admit I
have no effect
on morning, noon
or afternoon.

I'm not asking
who am I? I'm
asking if I'm
alive, if I'm
open with tears

working to my
existence, not
hoping one day
to walk the earth.
If I'm not dust,

dust I won't be.
This idea
is not true and
not false. If birth
lasts a lifetime,

the sun is glazed
with sunlight, is
its own nature,
each morning wants
itself to rise, body and sheen.

Renewal

Once a year, I listen hard
to Thelonious Monk playing
"I Love You I Love You
I Love You Sweetheart
Of All My Dreams," recorded

on October 6, 1964,
the day I was born,
the man sighing and squawking
and half-humming, his left
hand striding, his right hand

uniquely patchworking
together the melody.
I listen, really listen,
the sighing and the bird calling,
like half-speech before

language was created,
mixing together to form
a potion the keys just begin
to absorb, the melody like
a succession of first words.

Then I spend the next
364 days
progressively losing my focus
in constant anticipation
of getting it back.

Notes

"Prayer (1)" is based loosely on Allen Mandelbaum's translation of Salvatore Quasimodo's poem, "To the New Moon."

"Song (1): The two repeated lines, a few other images, and the overall structure, are borrowed from Mark Rudman and Bohdan Boychuk's translation of Boris Pasternak's poem, "English Lessons."

"Endless": The third part owes a great deal to Keith Jarrett's liner notes to his 1989 album, *Changeless*, with Gary Peacock and Jack DeJohnette. In addition, the title, and the subheading of the third part, is the title of the second track on that album.

"Keith Douglas 1920-1944": The epigraph is from Keith Douglas's poem, "Simplify Me When I'm Dead." The second quote is from the fragments of a poem Douglas planned to call "Bete Noire." The third quote is from Douglas's poem, "Words." All three poems can be found in Douglas's *The Complete Poems*, published by Oxford University Press.

"Stephen Crane In the Bowery": Crane's pre-*The Red Badge of Courage* impressionism, which this poem strives to illuminate and celebrate, is featured in his novel *Maggie: A Girl of the Streets*, as well as various stories, sketches, and journalism about early 1890s New York City.

"Wallace Stevens in New York City": Many of the details are borrowed from Wallace Stevens's journals, excerpts of which are included in Joan Richardson's *Wallace Stevens: The Early Years, 1879-1923*.

"Harmony": In a questionnaire Marcel Proust answered when he was in his teens, in the first part of his response to "Your favorite colour and flower," he wrote, "The beauty is not in the colours, but in their harmony."

"A Question": Stephen Spender's own version of his experience can be found in his book, *The 30s and After*. The last line is inspired, in part, by Spender's war poem, "Rejoice In the Abyss."

"The Nature of Statues": Many readers will no doubt notice the references, in the opening image, and its echo in the sixth stanza, of a famous moment in the first section of T.S. Eliot's "The Waste Land."

"Song (2)": The refrain is borrowed from Iris DeMent's song, "When My Mornin' Comes Around," which is on her 1996 album, *The Way I Should*.

About the Author

Douglas Nordfors was born in Seattle in 1964. He earned a BA from Columbia University, and an MFA in poetry from The University of Virginia, and has taught writing and literature at Milton Academy, The University of Virginia, James Madison University, Germanna Community College, and WriterHouse. Over the years, he has published poems in journals such as *Poet Lore*, *Poetry Northwest*, *The Iowa Review*, *Quarterly West*, *The Hampden-Sydney Poetry Review*, and many others. His first book of poetry, *Auras*, was published in 2008.

www.ingramcontent.com/pod-product-compliance
Lightning Source LLC
Chambersburg PA
CBHW052111070526
44584CB00017B/2438